first words
JAPANESE

タクシー

Illustrated by
Andy Mansfield & Sebastien Iwohn

hello

こんにちは
konnichiwa
(kon-ni-chi-wa)

ice cream

アイスクリーム
aisukuriimu
(ais-ku-ree-mu)

water

みず

mizu

(mi-zu)

supermarket

スーパーマーケット

sūpāmāketto

(soo-pah-mah-ket-to)

trolley

ショッピングカート
shoppingu kāto
(shop-pin-gu kah-to)

cat

ねこ

neko

(ne-ko)

bus

バス

basu
(ba-su)

dress

ワンピース

wanpiisu

(wan-pee-su)

dog

いぬ

inu

(i-nu)

banana

バナナ

banana

(ba-na-na)

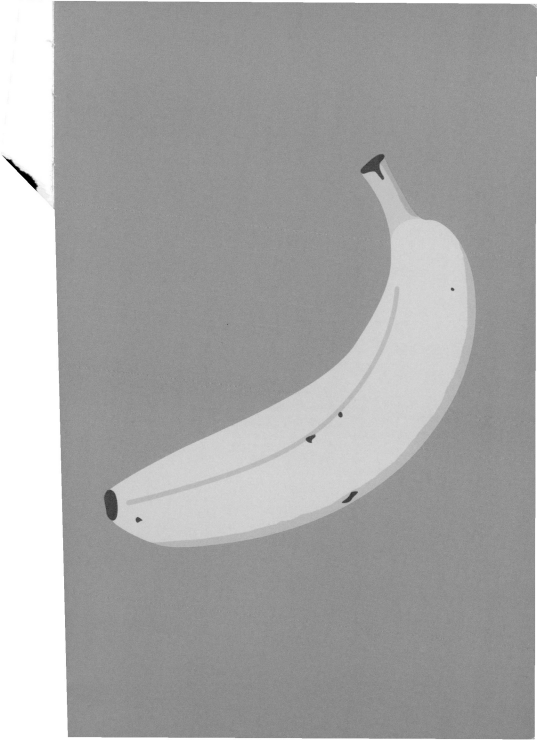

duck

かも

kamo

(ka-mo)

taxi

タクシー
takushii
(tak-shee)

duck

かも

kamo

(ka-mo)

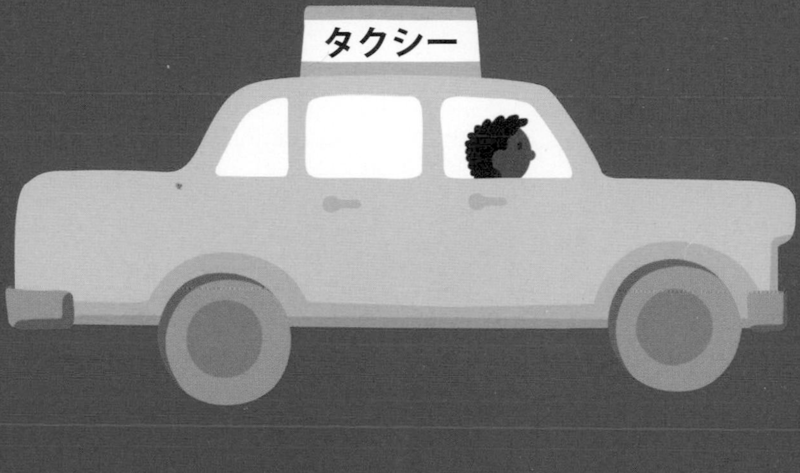
タクシー

t-shirt

ティーシャツ
tiishatsu
(tee-sha-tsu)

fish

さかな
sakana
(sa-ka-na)

aeroplane

ひこうき

hikōki

(hi-koh-ki)

chopsticks

はし
hashi
(ha-shi)

noodles

ラーメン

rāmen

(rah-men)

swimming pool
プール
pūru
(poo-ru)

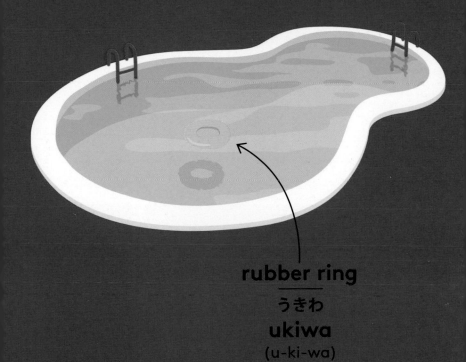

rubber ring

うきわ

ukiwa

(u-ki-wa)

cheese

チーズ

chiizu

(chee-zu)

bowl

ボウル
bōru
(boh-ru)

doctor

おいしゃさん
oishasan
(oy-sha-san)

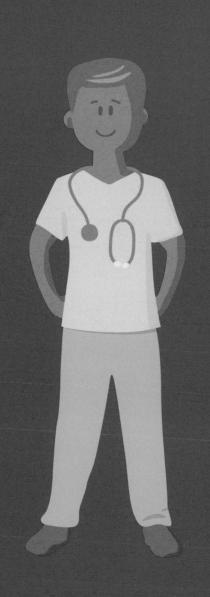

apple

りんご
ringo
(rin-go)

worm
—
むし
mushi
(mu-shi)

beach

ビーチ

biichi

(bee-chi)

bicycle

じてんしゃ
jitensha
(ji-ten-sha)

airport

くうこう
kūkō
(koo-koh)

juice

ジュース

jūsu

(joo-su)

market

いちば
ichiba
(i-chi-ba)

shoes

くつ

kutsu

(ku-tsu)

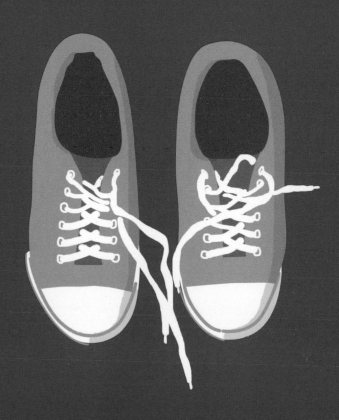

phone

でんわ

denwa

(den-wa)

post office

ゆうびんきょく

yūbinkyoku

(yoo-bin-kyo-ku)

restaurant

レストラン

resutoran

(res-to-ran)

hotel

ホテル

hoteru

(ho-te-ru)

milk

ぎゅうにゅう

gyūnyū

(gyoo-nyoo)

chocolate

チョコレート

chokorēto
(cho-ko-ray-to)

car

くるま
kuruma
(ku-ru-ma)

hat

ぼうし
bōshi
(boh-shi)

sunglasses

サングラス

sangurasu

(san-gu-ra-su)

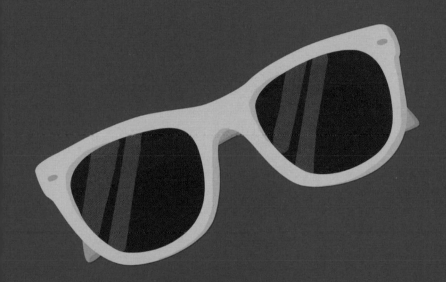

chicken

チキン
chikin
(chi-kin)

train

でんしゃ
densha
(den-sha)

station

えき

eki

(e-ki)

clock
とけい
tokei
(to-kay)

toilet

トイレ
toire
(toy-re)

bed

ベッド
beddo
(bed-do)

house

いえ

ie

(ih-eh)

chimney

えんとつ

entotsu

(en-to-tsu)

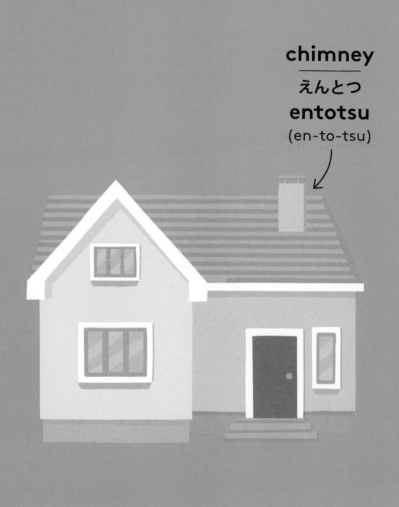

trousers

ズボン

zubon

(zu-bon)

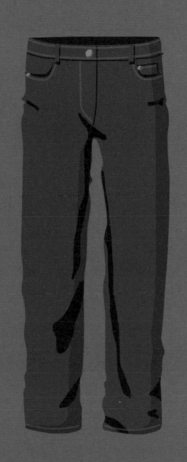

suitcase

スーツケース

sūtsukēsu

(soots-kay-su)

plate

さら

sara

(sa-ra)

knife

ナイフ

naifu

(nai-fu)

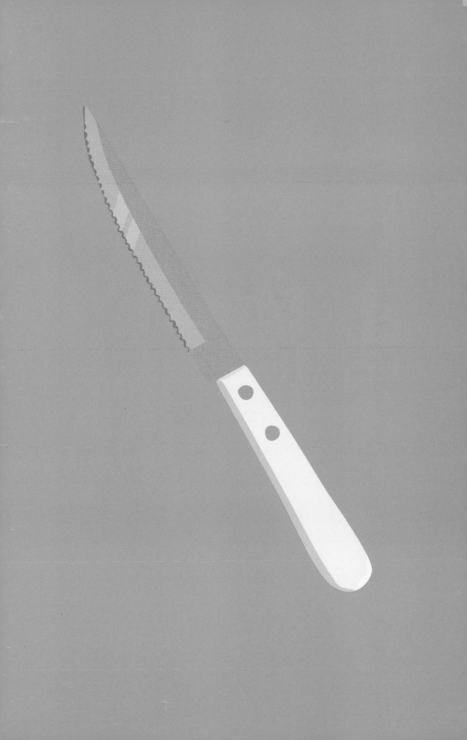

fork

フォーク
fōku
(foh-ku)

spoon

スプーン

supūn
(s-poon)

computer

コンピューター

konpyūtā

(kon-pyoo-tah)

mouse

マウス

mausu

(mau-su)

book

ほん

hon

(hon)

sandwich

サンドイッチ

sandoitchi

(san-doh-it-chi)

yes

はい

hai

(hai)

no

いいえ

iie

(ee-eh)

cinema

えいがかん

eigakan

(ay-ga-kan)

えいがかん

park

こうえん

kōen

(koh-en)

menu

メニュー

menyū

(men-yoo)

passport

パスポート

pasupōto

(pas-paw-toh)

police officer

おまわりさん

omawarisan

(o-ma-wa-ri-san)

key

かぎ

kagi

(ka-gi)

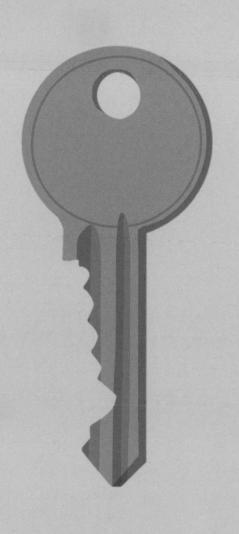

ticket

きっぷ

kippu

(kip-pu)

sushi

すし

sushi

(su-shi)

rain

あめ

ame

(a-meh)

snow

ゆき

yuki

(yu-ki)

sun

たいよう
taiyō
(tai-yoh)

tree

き

ki

(ki)

flower

はな

hana

(ha-na)

cake

ケーキ

kēki
(kay-ki)

cherry

さくらんぼ
sakuranbo
(sa-ku-ram-bo)

ball

ボール
bō-ru
(boh-ru)

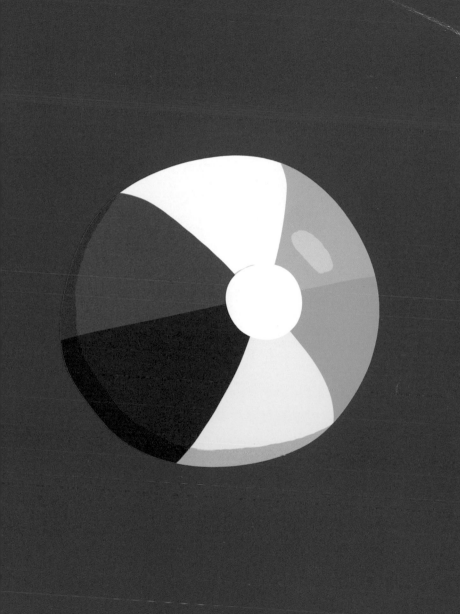

bird

とり

tori

(to-ri)

egg

たまご

tamago

(ta-ma-go)

umbrella

かさ

kasa

(ka-sa)

panda

パンダ

panda

(pan-da)

money

おかね

okane

(o-ka-ne)

bank

ぎんこう
ginkō
(gin-koh)

mouse

ねずみ

nezumi

(ne-zu-mi)

scarf

マフラー

mafurā
(ma-fu-rah)

gloves

てぶくろ

tebukuro

(te-bu-ku-ro)

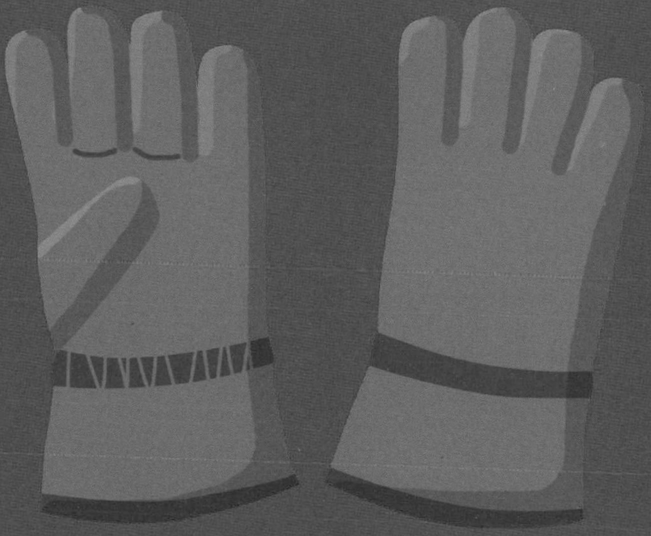

coat

コート

kōto

(koh-to)

hospital

びょういん

byōin

(byoh-in)

chair

いす
isu
(i-su)

table

テーブル
tēburu
(tay-bu-ru)

toothbrush

はブラシ

haburashi
(ha-bu-ra-shi)

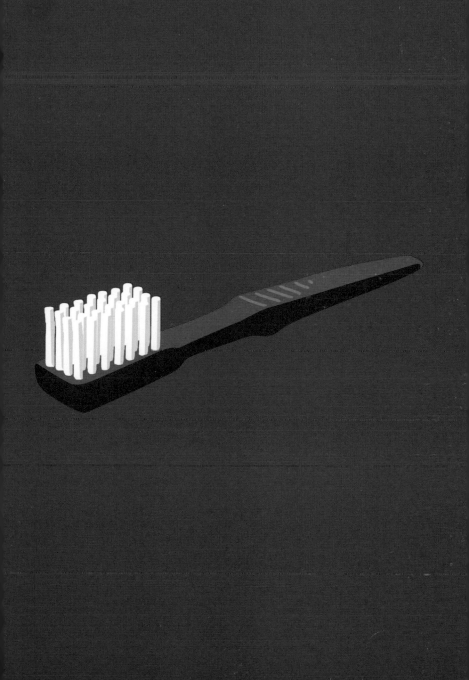

toothpaste

はみがきこ
hamigakiko
(ha-mi-ga-ki-ko)

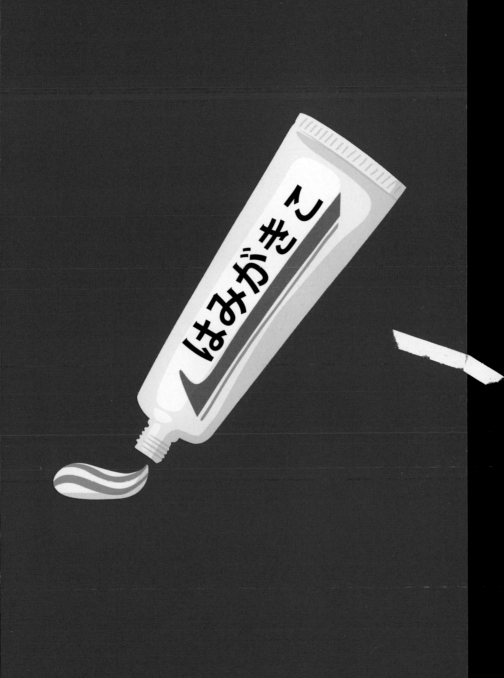

sun cream

ひやけどめ

hiyakedome

(hi-ya-ke-do-me)

spf 50

lion

ライオン

raion

(rai-on)

mountain

ーー

やま

yama

(ya-ma)

monkey

さる

saru

(sa-ru)

spider

くも

kumo

(ku-mo)

rice

——

ごはん

gohan

(go-han)

pen

ペン

pen
(pen)

door

ドア
do-a
(do-a)

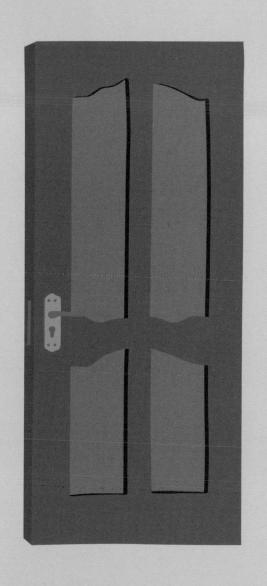

window

まど

mado
(ma-do)

curtain
カーテン
kāten
(kah-ten)

tent

テント
tento

(ten-to)

map

ちず

chizu

(chi-zu)

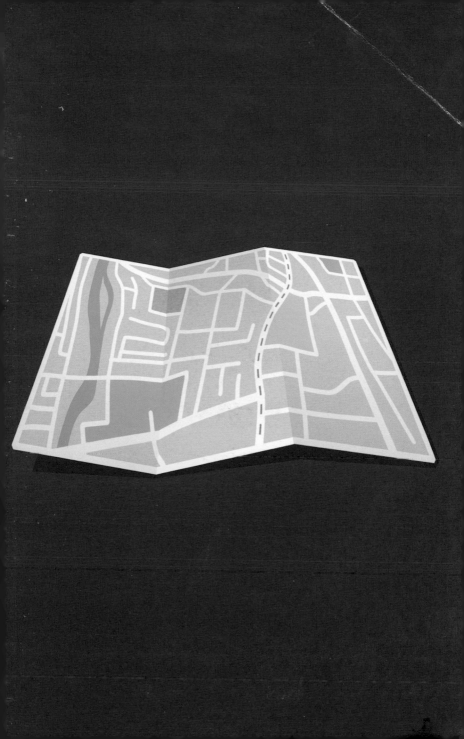

tomato

トマト

tomato

(to-ma-to)

moon

つき

tsuki

(ts-ki)

stars

ほし

hoshi
(ho-shi)

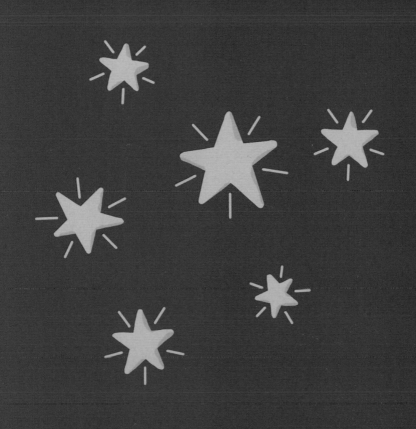

postcard

___

はがき

hagaki

(ha-ga-ki)

stamp

きって

kitte

(kit-te)

boat

———

ふね

fune

(fu-ne)

goodbye

さようなら

sayōnara

(sa-yoh-na-ra)